THE BACHELORETTE 2022:

Interesting Reviews On The American Reality Show.

By Ruby Styles

Table Of Contents

Chapter 1: What is The Bachelorette 2022 all about this season!

For the first time in the long-handling show's history, this season of The Bachelor will see two lovely ladies, Gabby Windey and Rachel Recchia, searching for their perfect man contemporaneously.

The brace preliminarily starred together on The Bachelor when Clayton Echard was the star of the season and although they may not have set up love(as Clayton ultimately chose to pursue a love with Susie Evans) they snappily stole the hearts of The Bachelorette suckers.

Gabby Windey and Rachel Recchia are on the hunt for their dream man on" The Bachelor" 2022.

Gabby Windey

Gabby Windey is one of this time's Bachelorettes on a veritably special series of" The Bachelor".

Gabby, 31, is a former NFL cheerleader and registered nanny from Denver, Colorado.

Rachel Recchia

Rachel Recchia is starring in a veritably special season of" The Bachelor".

Rachel, 26, from Chicago, is a marketable airman and flight educator.

Gabby and Rachel have a cast of 32 suitors who'll be fighting for their affections when the new season hits our defenses.

Meet the men of The Bachelorette 2022.

Logan

Logan is a 26- time-old videographer from San Diego.

Alec

Will Alec find love on" The Bachelor" 2022?

Alec, 27, is a marriage shooter from Houston, Texas.

Joey

Joey has joined the cast of" The Bachelor" 2022.

Joey, 24, is starring in the show with his binary family Justin.

Justin B

Another Justin on the cast of" The Bachelor" 2022.

Justin B, 32, is a physical therapist from California.

Zach

Will Zach find love on" The Bachelor" in 2022?

Zach, 25, is a tech superintendent from California.

John

John has joined the cast of" The Bachelor" 2022.

John, 26, is an English schoolteacher from Nashville, Tennessee.

Nate

Will Nate find love on" The Bachelor" 2022?

Nate, 33, is an electrical mastermind from Chicago.

Jason

Jason is looking to win Rachel or Gabby's heart on" The Bachelor" 2022.

Jason is a 30- time-old investment banker from Santa Monica, California.

Erich

suckers will see Erich on their defenses when" The Bachelor" returns.

Erich, 29, is a real estate critic from New Jersey.

Jacob

Jacob is ready for" The Bachelor" 2022.

Jacob, 27, is a mortgage broker from Scottsdale, Arizona.

Roby

suckers will see Roby on their defenses when" The Bachelor" returns.

Magician Roby, 33, hails from Los Angeles, California.

Tino

Tino is ready for" The Bachelor" 2022.

Tino, 28, is a general contractor from California.

Chris

Chris is looking for love on" The Bachelor" 2022. Intelligence trainer Chris, 30, is from Redondo Beach, California.

Spencer

Spencer has joined the cast of" The Bachelor" 2022.Spencer, 27, is an army officer from Chicago.

Brandan

Brandan is looking for love on" The Bachelor" 2022. Bartender Brandan, from California, is 23.

Aven

Will Aven catch Rachel or Gabby's attention on" The Bachelor" 2022?. Aven, 28, is a deals superintendent from San Diego.

Michael

Michael has joined the cast of" The Bachelor" 2022. Michael, 32, is a pharmaceutical salesperson from Long Beach, California.

James

" The Bachelor" 2022 has James on the cast. Meatball sucker James, 25, is from Winnetka, Illinois.

Justin Y

" The Bachelor" 2022 has Justin Y on the cast. Justin is starring in the show with his binary family.

Ryan

Ryan is ready for" The Bachelor" 2022.

Ryan, 36, is an investment director from Boston, Massachusetts.

Jordan V

" The Bachelor" suckers will see Jordan on their defenses. Jordan V, 27, is a drag racer from Alpharetta, Georgia.

Hayden

Hayden has joined the cast of" The Bachelor" 2022. 29- time-old rest superintendent Hayden is from Tampa, Florida.

Jordan H

Another Jordan on" The Bachelor" 2022 cast. Jordan H, 35, is a software inventor and also hails from Tampa, Florida.

Matt

Matt is hoping to catch Rachel or Gabby's eye on" The Bachelor" 2022. Matt, 25, is a shipping superintendent from San Diego.

Tyler

Tyler will be looking for love on" The Bachelor" 2022. Small business proprietor Tyler, 25, is from New Jersey.

Mario

Mario has joined the cast of" The Bachelor" 2022. Mario, 31, is a particular coach from Naperville, Illinois.

Colin

Colin is looking for love on" The Bachelor" 2022. Colin, 36, is a deals director from Chicago.

Ethan

Ethan has joined the cast of" The Bachelor" 2022. Ethan, 27, is an advertising superintendent from New York.

Quincey

Will Quincey be successful on" The Bachelor" 2022?. Quincey, 25, is a life trainer from Miami, Florida.

Johnny

Will Johnny find love on" The Bachelor" 2022? Johnny, 25, is a realtor from Florida.

Kirk

Kirk has joined the cast of" The Bachelor" 2022. College football trainer Kirk, 29, is from Texas.

Tremayne

Tremayne is ready for" The Bachelor" 2022.Tremayne, 28, from Naperville, Illinois, works in crypto.

Chapter 2:Hot Trends on The Bachelorette 2022

Who is Hosting The Bachelorette 2022?

Former Bachelor Jesse Palmer will return to host The Bachelor Season 19.

The star, who appeared on The Bachelor himself back in 2004, made his hosting debut during the last season of the manly-fronted series so no mistrustfulness suckers are looking forward to seeing him reunite with Gabby and Rachel.

The 2022 season of The Bachelor is the first two point two leading ladies contemporaneously. So far, the unknown season has had some drama, confusion, and hurt passions. still, Rachel Recchia and Gabby Windey have worked together to make the season a positive experience for each other. The Bachelorettes lately bandied whether they suppose The Bachelor could follow suit.

Rachel Recchia and Gabby Windey during the 2022 season of The Bachelor.

Rachel and Gabby wear marriage dresses.

Rachel and Gabby came close to musketeers during Clayton's season of ' The Bachelor '

Rachel and Gabby were musketeers before starring in the 2022 season of The Bachelor. The women were both rivals on Clayton Echard's season of The Bachelor.

In the end, Clayton broke up with both Rachel and Gabby to pursue Susie Evans, who left the show because Clayton told all three women that he loved them, and he was intimate with both Rachel and Gabby.

After the heartbreaking end to their time on The Bachelor, Rachel and Gabby came the 2022 Bachelorettes. The brace came veritably near during their time on The Bachelor, and they attribute their fellowship to the success of season 19.

The Bachelorettes answer whether the ballot could have two men lead ‘ The Bachelor ’

During an interview with Extra TV’s Billy Bush, Rachel and Gabby bandied rephotographing the 2022 season of The Bachelor. The brace was asked if they believed the same format could work for The Bachelor.

“ I suppose we say it can surely work, but the two guys would have to be as close and as open as Gabby and I both are for it to work, ” Rachel responded. “ You have to have that open line of communication else, it would just be going, I suppose, in a fully different direction. ”

Still, it would take a fully different path than what we took, ” Gabby added, “ If you want it to be easy and successful as a fellowship but if you didn’t put the other person first. “ So it’d be a different show. I don’t suppose you could compare it to what we did. ”

Gabby and Rachel maintained their fellowship while rephotographing ‘ The Bachelor ’ 2022

Although the first many weeks of The Bachelorette 2022 were rough for both Rachel and Gabby, it seems that the brace was in no way in conflict with each other. “ We didn’t have time to prepare or know what we were walking into, ” Gabby told Distractify in an interview. “ But we did know how important we love and admire each other and that fellowship would always come first. ”

While there were some bumps in the road, in week 3, the Bachelorettes decided to resolve the men into separate groups. Going forward, Rachel and Gabby will continue their separate journeys with their group of men.

" The Bachelor" 2022 rivals Gabby, Rachel

Each season, Bachelor Nation is introduced to a more dramatic(and seductive) cast than the last.

And The Bachelorette 2022 rivals for Gabby and Rachel's season are no exception.

Gabby Windey, a 31- time-old ICU nanny from O'Fallon, Illinois, and Rachel Recchia, a 26-time-old flight educator from Clermont, Florida, were rivals on The Bachelor season 26 with Clayton Echard, where they were both excluded from the final three after Clayton chose Susie Evans, a 29- time-old marriage videographer from Virginia Beach, Virginia, as his winner. Gabby and Rachel have blazoned as the season 19 Bachelorettes at The Bachelor season 26 " After the Final Rose " special in March 2022.

The Bachelor season 19 will be the first Bachelorette or Bachelor season to have two full-time leads. The Bachelor season 11 started with two Bachelorettes, Kaitlyn Bristowe and Britt Nilsson, but Kaitlyn was chosen as the sole Bachelor by the rivals in occasion one.

" It was a huge literacy process for everyone because it was a similar new home, " Gabby told People in July 2022. " But the experience Rachel and I had as Bachelorettes was so special and memorable. I don’t suppose we'd have had it any other way. ” She continued, “ I suppose people do know at this point that we do each have our own love stories. Of course, it was so nice to have each other to lean on and have that erected-in support as we were moving through. ” Rachel added, “ It’s just really amazing. We both get to have our peregrinations and our own stories, but still have each other along the way. ”

Rachel also verified to People that there won’t be any drama between her and Gabby on The Bachelor season 19 due to their constant “ communication ” through the process. “ I suppose Gabby and I just went into it talking to each other and knowing that throughout everything, we just had to have communication, ” she said. “ And that just worked for us throughout the whole thing. ” Gabby added, “ I suppose going in, knowing a little bit about it from Clayton’s season and stuff, I feel like we both had the station to put each other first. We know each other the stylish, our relationship above all is the most important. Plus a man that's worth it isn't going to have us fight over him, nor would we ever compromise our relationship for it. "

She continued, " It's only natural to be attracted to the same guys, then and there. We're mortal, but it would no way be anything that Rachel and I couldn't figure out on our own, especially always putting our relationship in the van of everything. "

As for how their season ends, Gabby and Rachel verified that they're happy with the outgrowth. " I suppose we feel good actually. And you learn so importantly about yourself going through this. So I feel like eventually, it's just an amazing life experience together, " Gabby said.
Rachel added, " I suppose we're both so thankful to have been given this and to be there together. We're both just really happy. "

But back to The Bachelorette 2022 rivals.

So who's in The Bachelor season 19 cast? Read on for what we know about The Bachelorette 2022 rivals for Gabby and Rachel's season, and what they want in a woman. From a magician to a brace of halves to a racecar motorist, The Bachelorette 2022 rivals are bones
to watch.

Fun data about Gabby listed the following

• Gabby is scarified of humpback jumbos but would love to see one in person from a safe distance.

• Gabby loves to write cards.

• Stomping grapes in Italy are at the top of Gabby's pail list.

Clayton also wasn't Gabby's first Bachelor Nation relationship. Gabby is the ex-girlfriend of both Dean Unglert from The Bachelor season 13 with Rachel Lindsay and Blake Horstmann from

The Bachelor season 14 with Becca Kufrin. Dean, who also starred on Bachelor in Paradise seasons 5 and 6, verified the relationship on an occasion of his " Help! I stink at Dating " podcast in October 2021. " She was, like, one of the main spouses. She was my gal from the council, " he said. " Directors called me and were like, ' Hey, we're thinking of casting this person — what do you suppose of her? We know that you dated 10 times agone. ' And I was like, ' Oh, she's great. However, she'll either win the show or she'll be the coming Bachelor, If she gets named for the show. ' And I forcefully believe that. "

Blake, who was also on Bachelor in Paradise season 6, also verified that he dated Gabby for a " couple months " on an occasion of the " Behind the Rose " podcast in October 2021. " We like the same girls, man. I didn't know Dean until obviously, like, 2018, but Gabby was a good friend of one of my veritably good musketeers from the council, they were roommates, " he said. " I met Gabby long before

I was on The Bachelor, like, I want to say perhaps 2015 or 2016. We hung out for a little bit, so I know her veritably well. And Dean, I don't know how it came up, but one time, I and Dean were sitting there I suppose we were in Buffalo, and he mentioned Gabby — and I was like, ' How do you know Gabby? ' And he was like, ' Dude, she was, like, my girl in council, you know, we were in love and boredom. '"
He continued, " She's fun. She has a veritably gregarious personality, veritably loud, like, when she walks into a room, you know she's in a room. You no way know if the lead is going to be into a commodity like that. You no way know if they like the further shy, quiet type or they like the loud, gregarious type, but she's surely veritably loud, veritably gregarious, she has a lot of musketeers. So if Clayton's into that, I see her getting motherlands, for sure. She's a beautiful woman. They're gonna have the football player, cheerleader storyline. "

" The Bachelor" 2022 Rachel

So who's The Bachelor 2022, Rachel Recchia? Rachel listed her job on The Bachelor as a " Flight educator. " Her Instagram bio also lists her job as an airman, as well as her Instagram handle@pilot. rachel. According to her Instagram, Rachel has flown to locales like Columbus, Ohio; Athens, Ohio; Springfield, Missouri; and Lakeland, Florida. She also attended Ohio University in Athens, Ohio, where she was a cheerleader.

In her Bachelorette memoir, Rachel described herself as a " hopeless romantic " who's looking for someone " nurturing, compassionate " and " regardful. " " Rachel is an intrepid frequent leaflet looking for a man who'll travel the world with her, " her memoir reads. " After lately earning her private airman license, the future is nothing but sunny skies ahead for Rachel and now she's hoping to find a pilot that matches her sense of adventure. As a hopeless romantic, Rachel is looking for someone who's as sportful, passionate, and robotic as she is. He should be nurturing, and compassionate and MUST be regardful in all angles of life – to her, to family, and especially to waitpersons. In the end, Rachel wants to find crazy, insane love that makes sense to no bone

differently but her and her soul mate. ”

Fun Data About Rachel listed the following

• Rachel could live off of Flaming Hot Cheetos.

• Rachel can't stay to read the Harry Potter series with her kiddies one day.

• Rachel formerly organized a flash mob in the high academy

Who's The Bachelor 2022 host?

Jesse Palmer," The Bachelor"

The Bachelor season 19 host is Jesse Palmer, who was the season 5 Bachelorette in 2004 and was the youthful Bachelorette in Bachelor Nation history at 24 times old. Jesse hosted his first Bachelorette ballot show in 2022 with The Bachelor season 26 with Clayton Echard. During The Bachelor season 5 homestretch, Jesse gave his Final Rose to Jessica Bowlin but didn't propose to her. Jesse and Jessica continued to date but ended their relationship many weeks after the homestretch of their Bachelorette season vented. In June 2020, Jesse and his gal, Emely Fardo, married in an intimate marriage in New York City. Jesse told Us Weekly in November 2021 that he and Emely planned to marry in Provence, France before the current health extremity canceled their marriage date. " We had firstly planned a marriage in Provence, France, for summer 2020, which was laid over until summer of 2021 due to the epidemic, but we didn't want to stay any longer, " he said at the time. " So, we had a small, private, and intimate form with close musketeers who lived in New York City. "

Jesse graduated from the University of Florida in Gainesville, Florida, where he played football for the Florida Gators, in 2001 with a bachelorette's of trades degree in political wisdom and a bachelorette's of wisdom degree in marketing. After scale, Jesse was drafted by the National Football League to play for the

New York Titans. He played with the platoon for four seasons from 2001 to 2005 as a quarterback. After the New York Titans, Jesse was drafted by the Canadian Football League to play for the Montreal Alouettes. He played with the platoon until 2005 when he was inked by the San Francisco 49ers. He also abnegated with the Montreal Alouettes in 2006 before he retired from football in 2007 to pursue a broadcasting career. Since his broadcasting career started, Jesse has worked with networks like Fox, NFL Network, ESPN, ABC, and SEC Network. He's also guest starred on Law & Order Special Victims Unit and made guest appearances on shows like form to Riches and Good Morning America, and hosted the Food Network's Spring Baking Championship and Holiday Baking Championship.

Jesse was blazoned as The Bachelor season 26 host in September 2021. " For further than 20 times, The Bachelor has brought the world dozens of indelible love stories, including at one time, my own, " he said at the time. " Falling in love is one of life’s topmost gifts, and I'm lowered by the occasion to return to the show as host this season to offer the newest Bachelorette advice gained from immediate experience and I'm thankful to play a small part in his trip. ” The advertisement came after Chris Harrison, the former host of Bachelor Nation, verified in June 2021 that he'd retired as the ballot’s host after 19 times. “ I ’ve had a truly inconceivable run as host of The Bachelor ballot and now I ’m agitated to start a new chapter, ” he wrote in an Instagram post at the time. “ I’m so thankful to Bachelor Nation for all of the recollections we’ve made together. While my two-decade trip is belting up, the gemütlichkeit I’ve made will last a continuance. ”

Deadline reported at the time that Chris entered an amid-range, eight-figure agreement as part of an exit plan with ABC, the network that airs the Bachelor ballot, and Warner Bros. TV, the company that produces the Bachelorette shows. The magazine also reported that Harrison’s agreement included a nondisclosure agreement.

Chris ' decision to retire as Bachelor Nation's host came after he was slammed for his response to season 25 Bachelorette competitor Rachael Kirkconnell's racism reproach in February 2021. Rachael, the winner of Matt James ' season, faced counterreaction at the time when prints resurfaced of her at an Old South Antebellum-themed party at Georgia College in 2018. Before the filmland went viral, Rachael was formerly under contestation after her former high academy classmate indicted her on TikTok for bullying her and other scholars for dating Black men. Other TikTok druggies also exposed Rachael for liking social media prints of her musketeers in culturally asleep costumes and with Belligerent flags.

Chris came under contestation after he was canvassed about the reproach by season 13 Bachelor Rachel Lindsay on Extra. During the interview, Chris asked suckers to give Rachael " grace " and explained that he didn't find the Antebellum party prints obnoxious because they just looked like filmland a council pupil takes at a party. Harrison also questioned whether the prints would be considered racially asleep in 2018 when they were taken. After the interview, numerous suckers slammed Harrison and indicted him of excusing Rachael's geste

.

ABC verified in March 2021 that Chris wouldn't host season 17 of The Bachelor and would be replaced by Tayshia and Kaitlyn. " Chris Harrison won't be hosting the coming season of The Bachelor, " ABC said in a statement at the time. " We support Chris in the work that he's committed to doing. In his absence, former Bachelorettes Tayshia Adams and Kaitlyn Bristowe will support the new Bachelor through the coming season. As we continue the dialogue around achieving lesser equity and addition within The Bachelor ballot, we're devoted to perfecting the BIPOC representation of our crew, including among the administrative patron species. These are an important way of effecting abecedarian change so that our ballot is a festivity of love that's reflective of our world. ” He officially retired as the Bachelor Nation’s host in June 2021.

The Bachelor airs on Mondays at 8 p.m. on ABC and is available to sluice on Hulu. Then’s how to watch it for free.

Chapter 3: Spoiler Alerts!

SPOILER! What happens to Logan on The Bachelorette 2022?

What happens to Logan on The Bachelorette 2022? Logan doesn't win The Bachelor 2022 and doesn’t admit a Final Rose from either Gabby or Rachel. On occasion 5 of The Bachelor season 19, Logan flips from Rachel to Gabby. On occasion 3 of Gabby and Rachel’s Bachelor season, Rachel offers Logan a rose to be her competitor, which he accepts. still, according to Reality Steve, Logan ends up changing his mind latterly in the season, when he tells Rachel that he has a stronger passion for Gabby and becomes Gabby’s competitor rather. Reality Steve reports that Logan’s switch doesn’t beget any drama between Gabby and Rachel and that Gabby eliminates Logan before Hometown Dates.

For his limo preface on occasion 1 of The Bachelor season 19, Logan introduced himself to Gabby and Rachel by holding two sprats in his hands. " Before I meet you, I want to introduce you to a couple of my musketeers. When I heard there were going to be two Bachelorettes, I figured I should exercise hanging out with a couple of sprats all the time. So then they are, " Logan said. " This is Mary Beth. This is Alejandra. Alejandra has a station, but she's doing OK now. My name is Logan. "

Logan is also a competitor on Bachelor in Paradise season 8, alongside Bachelor season 19 rivals Jacob Rapini, a 27- time-old mortgage broker from Scottsdale, Arizona; Johnny DeFilippo, a 25- time-old realtor from Palm Beach auditoriums, Florida; Tyler Norris, a 25-time-old small business proprietor from Wildwood, New Jersey; Hayden Markowitz, a 29- time-old rest superintendent from Tampa, Florida; and Joey and Justin Young, 24- time-old halves from Brookfield, Connecticut.

Jacob, Johnny, and Logan are a part of the original Bachelorette in Paradise season 8 cast who arrive on day one. Three rivals from Gabby and Rachel's season made it to the end of Bachelor in Paradise season 8 Logan, Tyler, and Johnny. At the end of Bachelor in Paradise season 8, Logan and Kate Gallivan, a competitor from The Bachelor season 26 with Clayton Echard, broke up; Tyler and Brittany Galvin, a competitor from The Bachelor season 25 with Matt James, didn't get engaged but left together; and Johnny and Victoria Fuller, a competitor from The Bachelor season 24 with Peter Weber, got engaged.

SPOILER Who does Gabby pick as The Bachelorette 2022 winner?

Who does Gabby pick as The Bachelorette 2022 winner? While he doesn't know Gabby's winner, Reality Steve verified that Gabby's final three include Erich Schwer, a 29- time-old real estate critic from Bedminster, New Jersey; Jason

Alabaster, a 30- time-old investment banker from Santa Monica, California. He also believed that Justin Budfuloski, a 32- time-old physical therapist from Solana Beach, California, was also likely in Gabby's final three, but that turned out to be incorrect because Justin was excluded in Rose Ceremony# 2. Reality Steve verified that Gabby excluded her fourth-place finalist, Johnny DeFilippo, a 25- time-old realtor from Palm Beach auditoriums, Florida, after Hometown Dates. Johnny is also on Bachelor in Paradise season 8, where he got engaged to Victoria Fuller from The Bachelor season 24 with Peter Weber.

Reality Steve also verified that The Bachelor season 19 homestretch and Fantasy Suite dates were mugged in Mexico. TikTok account@zacharyreality also verified in July 2022 that both Gabby and Rachel get engaged in The Bachelor season 19 homestretch. " Gabby and Rachel will both be getting engaged this season on The Bachelor. I would no way, ever say who it is, especially without a warning, but I'll confirm there will be two rings, " Zachary

Reality said. For Gabby's engagement, it's nearly certain that the ring was designed by Neil Lane, a celebrity jeweler, who has created engagement rings for The Bachelor, The Bachelorette, and Bachelor in Paradise since 2008. In a 2016 interview with Entertainment Weekly, former host Chris Harrison revealed that Bachelor Nation couples have to stay together for a certain quantum of time, else they've to return the free engagement ring to Neil Lane. " There's some rule, after a certain number of times, you get to keep it anyway, " he said. " But after months it goes back. "

Lane told StyleCaster in 2016 that he doesn't know where the rings go, but that he designs them with the stopgap that the couple stays together. " I make rings hoping that people stay together ever, but after they get the ring, I don't have a say-so in it, and what happens after that, I don't know, " he said. " Where the ring goes, I've to say, I don't know. I just say it goes to ring heaven. "

Before The Bachelor season 19 homestretch, Gabby had Hometown Dates with her final four, which included Erich, Jason, and Johnny. For Gabby's Hometown Date with Jason in New Orleans, Louisiana, they went to the French Quarter, walked by Jackson Square, and threw globules from a deck at the bar, Saints, and wrongdoers, possessed by Channing Tatum. For Gabby's Hometown Date with Johnny in North Palm Beach, Florida, they went to Johnny's parent's house. They also had a date in Jupiter, Florida, where they visited Jupiter Beach Park. For Gabby's Hometown Date with Erich in Bedminster, New Jersey, they visited Natirar Park and Erich's family's house.

SPOILER Who does Rachel pick as The Bachelorette 2022 winner?

Who does Rachel pick as The Bachelorette 2022 winner? While he doesn't know Rachel's winner, Reality Steve verified that Rachel's final two are Zach Shallcross, a 25- time-old tech superintendent from Anaheim Hills, California;

and Tino Franco, a 27- time-old general contractor from Playa del Ray, California. Reality Steve verified that Rachel excluded her third-place finalist, Aven Jones, a 28- time-old deals superintendent from San Diego, California, after Fantasy Suites. He also verified that Rachel excluded her fourth-place finalist, Tyler Norris, a 25- time-old small business proprietor from Wildwood, New Jersey, after Hometown Dates. Tyler is also on Bachelor in Paradise season 8, where he ends up with Brittany Galvin, a competitor from The Bachelor season 25 with Matt James. Reality Steve also verified that The Bachelor season 19 homestretch and Fantasy Suite dates were mugged in Mexico.

Reality Steve also verified that The Bachelor season 19 homestretch and Fantasy Suite dates were mugged in Mexico. TikTok account@zacharyreality also verified in July 2022 that both Rachel and Gabby get engaged in The Bachelor season 19 homestretch. For Rachel's engagement, it's nearly certain that the ring was designed by Neil Lane, a celebrity jeweler, who has created engagement rings for The Bachelor, The Bachelorette, and Bachelor in Paradise since 2008. In a 2016 interview with Entertainment Weekly, former host Chris Harrison revealed that Bachelor Nation couples have to stay together for a certain quantum of time, else they've to return the free engagement ring to Neil Lane. “ There’s some rule, after a certain number of times, you get to keep it anyway, ” he said. “ But after months it goes back. ”

Lane told StyleCaster in 2016 that he doesn’t know where the rings go, but that he designs them with the stopgap that the couple stays together. “ I make rings hoping that people stay together ever, but after they get the ring, I don’t have a say-so in it, and what happens after that, I don’t know, ” he said. “ Where the ring goes, I've to say, I don’t know. I just say it goes to ring heaven. ”

www.ingramcontent.com/pod-product-compliance
Lightning Source LLC
LaVergne TN
LVHW020534160826
845677LV00015B/4058

* 9 7 9 8 8 4 5 8 4 0 8 8 2 *